Also by Jayne Martin

Tender Cuts
Suitable for Giving: A Collection of Wit
with a Side of Wry

The Daddy Chronicles

The Daddy Chronicles

JAYNE MARTIN

Whisk(e)y Tit
NYC & VT

Published in the United States by Whisk(e)y Tit: www.whiskeytit.com. If you wish to use or reproduce all or part of this book for any means, please let the author and publisher know. You're pretty much required to, legally.

ISBN 978-1-952600-25-8

Cover design: Miette Gillette

For all

the fatherless

daughters

Contents

Praise   xiii

Prologue   xvii

1. The Other Woman   1

2. First Love   3

3. Pinball   5

4. And Then He Is Gone   7

5. Just Like Family   11

6. Where I Learn About God   13

7. Sam   15

8. Bless Me Father for I Have Sinned   17

9. Shifting Sands   19

10. Just Out of Reach   21

11. This Is Where We Live Now   23

12. The Man We've Married   25

13. Mood Swings   27

14. Just Like Marilyn Monroe   29

15. Another Thing Goes Missing   31

16. At the Stroke of Midnight   33

17. What We Want To Be   35

18. The Boy I Like   37

19. The Boy Who Likes Me   39

20. Fault Lines   41

21. Final Exit   43

22. Jayne with a "Y"   45

23. Condolences   47

24. What Boys Want   *49*

25. On My Own   *51*

26. Just Like In the Movies   *53*

27. The Dating Game   *55*

28. And Then There Were None   *57*

29. Unspoken   *59*

30. Madly in Love – Again   *61*

31. Cosmic Fluke   *65*

32. Implosion   *67*

33. That's A Wrap   *69*

34. Just Like Elizabeth Taylor   *71*

35. Father Figure   *73*

36. And Then We Are One   *77*

37. Seismic Shift   *79*

Acknowledgements   *83*

About the Author   *85*

About the Publisher   *87*

Praise

"The primal longing for wholeness is at the heart of *The Daddy Chronicles*, whose mosaic structure reflects Martin's fragmented family upbringing. Like too many, Martin grew up with an absent father. Brutally direct, hauntingly poetic, this memoir's emotional center is its compelling honesty and vulnerability." — Sue William Silverman, author, *How to Survive Death and Other Inconveniences*

"Disarming in its honesty, fierce in its longing, *The Daddy Chronicles* is the story of a girl without a father and the cost of unmet hunger. In a series of written snapshots, Jayne Martin provides a kaleidoscopic view into her childhood and grips the reader with raw and unflinching prose."

— Sonja Livingston, author, *Ghostbread*

"Don't let the length of the short stories in *The Daddy Chronicles* fool you. Martin poignantly captures the heart of a fatherless daughter through the many stages of loss that happen in a fatherless daughter's journey. The initial gut punch of grief in her words grab you, but it is her strength that keeps pulling you in. She, like all fatherless daughters before her, is a warrior who rises through the ashes and gives the reader the blueprint to follow suit in their own exploration of understanding and healing. Welcome to the tribe."

— Denna Babul, author, *The Fatherless Daughter Project: Understanding Our Losses and Reclaiming Our Lives and Love Strong: Change Your Narrative, Change Your Life and Take Your Power Back.*

"In a series of poignant and poetic vignettes, this memoir delivers the complexity of an entire lifetime on the head of a pin. While unflinching exploration of loss and longing drives the narrative forward, the destination is, ultimately, a place of reclamation–of memory, of agency, and of self. Martin's spare images crackle and resonate not only with the energy and impact of her experiences, but also with the quiet wisdom she has gleaned from them."
— Jeannine Ouellette, author, *The Part That Burns*

"This collection of priceless memories not only made me reflect on my own stories, but heal and grow from the beautiful words on the page. Everyone will relate to different parts of this poetic masterpiece."
— Gabrielle Stone, author of *"Eat, Pray, #FML"*

Prologue

Ode to the Lone Sperm

Eager little swimmer, perhaps my
competitive nature comes from you
Who didn't get the memo that
fertilization was not my father's intent
Content as he was to have my mother
all to himself, but you
You failed to notice your brethren sperm
treading water, not even trying
Trying to tell you to ease up little fella,
this guy's just going through the motions
Motions where emotions would never bloom,
and in your haste to win the race a child
Growing in the shadow of his withholding,
A child always wondering why.

1

The Other Woman

The other woman waits. It's what she does. She does not expect your sympathy. She knows she is the villain in this piece. At 19, you may say she was old enough to know better. At 40, he was a master of deceit. Charmed by the melody of his promises, she eagerly danced for his pleasure. Faster, he would say, and she would spin until, dizzy and exhausted, she would collapse only to find him gone once again.

Her dance shoes now scuffed, heels worn from years of tapping to his tune, leave her toes twisted and blistered. Another dinner abandoned on the stove. Filets she couldn't afford, withered and cold. The vodka numbs her senses as she drifts off to sleep, still dressed for seduction.

2

First Love

The baby sticks her chubby little arm through the bars of the playpen and squeals.

Look at me.

The father's eyes stay intent on the television.

The baby hoists herself up on tiptoes for the first time. Surprised and delighted with this new skill, she giggles, squeals louder, clinging to the bars with both hands.

Look at me!

The father gives her only a brief glance.

The baby reaches out with both arms, but as soon as she does she loses her balance and falls on her behind. She howls, her cheeks crimson, awash in tears.

The father turns up the sound on the television until it drowns out her cries.

3

Pinball

The child falls asleep to the fog horns of San Francisco, awakens to rain on a rooftop in Portland, snow on the ground in Bozeman, the high-desert heat of Carson City; a pinball bouncing from paddle to paddle at the hands of others. The landscapes blur as the train, the bus, the car rolls by. Glimpses of homes and families that are never her own as her mother attempts another reconciliation with her wandering father.

Alone, in one more strange bed, the baby doll she has named after herself held tightly to her chest, she calls out, "Mommy?"

Her bare feet pat their way along the wooden floor, down a hallway to a closed door. She stretches upward to the doorknob. Its cold steel fills her tiny palm. A turn and the door creaks open into a narrow, dimly-lit room. Against the wall to her left is a single metal-framed bed where her father lies facing away, her mother's arms wrapped tightly around his bare shoulders. He turns and looks down at her, then back at her mother.

"Get her out of here," he says.

Tilt.

4

And Then He Is Gone

When Daddy leaves us for the last time, he wears a blue pin-striped suit with a freshly-pressed handkerchief in his chest pocket, a fedora hat, and black oxfords that shine like new pennies. Tall, oh-so-handsome, he looks just like one of those movie stars that smile out from the covers of the magazines Mommy keeps on her vanity.

My small hands press against the

window. I draw a heart with my finger in the circle of my breath as I watch him carry his suitcase across the busy city street, growing smaller with each step he takes away from us. The bell of a cable car rings out as it passes by. And then he is gone, never having turned, never seeing me still waving long after he disappears. My heart melts and slides down the glass.

For weeks after that, I still ask, "When is Daddy coming home?" He had left us before. Left and came back. Left and came back. Upon each return, I would run into his arms, his embrace short and stiff, but enough for me to breathe in his scent, cloves and pine, capturing it in my memory like a firefly in a Mason jar.

"You knew he wasn't a family man when you married him," my grandmother says to my mother. But she is looking at me. And though I don't know what "family man" means, I see Mommy turn her head to hide her tears.

"When Daddy comes back, I'll be such a good girl. Such a good girl," I say.

My tummy starts to hurt and I crawl up into Daddy's chair, my bare legs sticking to the leather, my tiny bottom trying to fill the space left by his, and wonder what I could have done to make him stay.

5

Just Like Family

After bouncing from relative to relative, it's just Mommy and me. The morning sun warms our one-bedroom apartment where Mommy has put up curtains, white with daisies embroidered along the edges like those I pick from gardens. *He loves me. He loves me not.*

For the first time, I make friends. Every day after school I go play with Franny. Her large stone and brick house has kids hollering, running around, and hanging out of every window. There's always a big pitcher of Kool-Aid in their refrigerator. I can help myself, like I'm one of the family, and no one ever asks where my dad is.

Franny is the youngest. She has six older sisters and brothers and another baby is on the way. There's always another on the way. They're Catholic. And now so am I even though I don't really know what that means. Sometimes Franny still sucks her thumb.

We dig a big hole in the corner of her backyard. "All the way to China!" we shout. We climb a tree, sit on the lowest branch sucking on Pixy Stix. We talk about the movie stars we will marry, our houses next door to each other. Franny wants four kids. I don't want any.

There are tons of hiding places and hide-and-seek goes on for hours. Curled in the back of her parent's closet, I slip my feet inside her dad's slippers. I imagine never being found. Franny's mom telling mine, "I'm sorry. We looked and looked."

6

Where I Learn About God

In my maroon jumper, white blouse, and polished white oxfords, I look like every other first-grader at Saint Matthews Catholic School. And, like every other kid, it turns out I have a father named God "who art in heaven" a place we go when we die if we are good. Franny and I can't sit next to each other because we talk in class.That is not good. I learn the word *sin*. I learn the word *confession*. And that

God is watching. Always watching. I learn about praying where we can ask God for stuff. He's sounding more and more like Santa, except Santa usually brings me what I ask for. I pray and pray, but Daddy never calls.

7

Sam

Mommy's soft, blonde curls tickle her cheekbones. Her pale skin has a rosy glow, even by candlelight, and she always smells of City of Paris perfume.

She's had other boyfriends, but I like Sam the best. He always shows up with a present and takes me when they go places. Tonight I'm wearing a navy blue dotted-Swiss dress. My hair is in a pony tail that stretches all the way down my back. He tells me I look like a princess.

At the restaurant, everyone is dressed up. I am the only child there. A woman at the next table says to Mommy, "She's very well-mannered."

I sip on my Shirley Temple with the extra cherry feeling very grown up.

Later when Mommy tucks me into bed I protest, but only weakly. I know Mommy and Sam want some grown-up time. I suspect they will kiss and I try to stay awake to spy, but my tummy is full and soon the weight of my eyelids wins out. It seems I've been asleep for just a short time when I hear footsteps, but daylight is starting to peek through the blinds. Mommy walks through my room to get to the bathroom. She has no clothes on. Sam follows right behind her, his boy thing dangling between his legs. They close the bathroom door.

When they come out, I keep my eyes tightly shut.

8

Bless Me Father for I Have Sinned

Franny's mom drops me off after school so I can change out of my uniform to go play. Mommy is still at work, but I have my own key. When I open the door, it's dark inside. All the shades are pulled down like closed eyes.

"Hey, princess," says Sam.

He's lying on the sofa bed where Mommy sleeps, but it's never open in the daytime.

"I was just taking a nap." He scooches over a bit, pats the mattress. "Come keep me company."

This is the part of the movie where the audience is screaming at the screen, "Don't go down to the basement!"

On the screen in my head though are all the times I've seen Franny crawl into her dad's lap, watched them cuddle as he stroked her hair and kissed the top of her head, wanting so badly for it to be me his arms held.

I close the door behind me, hear the lock "click" into place.

"Maybe for just a minute," I say.

I nestle into the conclave of his chest like a tiny spoon as his body closes around mine, pulling me into his warmth. His breath tickling the tiny hairs on the back of my neck. I think *this must be love.* When he slips his hand inside my panties, I pretend to be asleep.

9

Shifting Sands

It turns out Sam wasn't "the marrying kind." I could have told Mommy other stuff about Sam, but I keep that locked tightly away where no one will ever find it.

The new boyfriend hasn't been around that long, but my grandmother likes him. I'm pretty sure she likes him more than Mommy does.

"He's a good match for you," she tells

Mommy. "And your daughter needs a real home."

"If you don't want me to marry him, I won't," Mommy says to me.

I am eight years old, and pretty sure that's not old enough to decide whether or not my mother should remarry.

The man is kind to her, good to me. But his shoes do not shine like my Daddy's.

I look into her eyes. They are green as the swirling sea. The floor pulls away from under my feet like sand in a riptide.

10

Just Out of Reach

In my dream, I'm wandering alone in a forest at the edge of an ocean. Pine trees so tall they seem to touch the sky. Waves crash against cliffs far below and the air tastes of salt. Something growls nearby. Fallen branches crack under the creature's weight as it moves in the shadows around me.

In the distance, I see the shape of a man shrouded in mist and though I can't make out his face I know it's my father. I'm running toward him, running, running. But I can never get any closer.

When I wake up I've wet the bed.

11

This Is Where We Live Now

"You can call me 'Dad,' if you want," says the-man-we've-married.

There's some talk about him adopting me, like I'm one of those kids on the plastic containers begging for money at the grocery store checkout.

"I already have a dad," I say.

We live in a two-bedroom house shaped like a box on a street named Cherry. I share a bedroom with the-girl-who-is-not-my-sister. She's six years older and does her best to ignore me.

We look like every other family on the block. Two grownups and two kids. A station wagon in the driveway. And a dog named Poncho, a mutt who humps everyone's legs. I love him.

I walk to school by myself, the new girl in my third grade public school class. No nuns. No uniforms. No crucifix needed. I know I'm a sinner.

"Say hello to Jane," the teacher says.

"Hello, Jane," the kids echo back, a sea of strangers.

The kid nobody likes offers to have lunch with me. I miss Franny.

I sleep on the top bunk. Sometimes I leave my body, float up through the ceiling, sit on the roof and stare at the stars. Daddy sits on the Big Dipper and waves to me.

12

The Man We've Married

The-man-we've-married has a face as round as the moon and blue eyes that crinkle when he smiles. He repairs roads, fixes broken water lines, and lays cement during the day. At night, he plays the violin.

The-man-we've-married fixes up an old box cart scooter, paints it black with a big white "Z" on the side for Zorro. He gives me and my friends rides all around the neighborhood, never says "no" to our pleas for "just once more."

The-man-we've-married takes us to Disneyland for my birthday. I get my picture taken with Cinderella.

The-man-we've-married teaches me to ice skate. His arm securely around my waist, we glide 'round and 'round the rink. *Swish-swish.* Our blades cut across the ice. He never lets me fall.

Still, I do not call him Dad.

13

Mood Swings

The-girl-who-is-not-my-sister hangs out in the backyard with her friends drinking Cokes. I wasn't invited. Neither was Poncho. The leg-humping thing.

When she was nine, the age I am now, her mother stepped in front of the train that runs on the tracks just up the block from this house. It wasn't an accident.

I listen for the blast of the train's horn

each day and watch Mommy carefully for mood swings.

Mommy says sometimes she can feel the woman's presence, her deep sadness within the walls.

14

Just Like Marilyn Monroe

Snip, snip go the scissors and my waist-long hair falls to the floor like roadkill.

My cousin says she'll let me see when she's all done. She's in beauty school so I expect I will be beautiful just like Marilyn Monroe.

"Hold still," my cousin says, as she cuts bangs. "I don't want to poke your eye out."

I've never had bangs before. Every day,

Mommy pulled my hair back from my face into a ponytail with me yelling, "Too tight! Too tight!"

"All done!" she says and holds up a mirror.

I don't look like Marilyn at all. I look like I have a bowl on my head. Like the kid on the Dutch Boy paint can.

Hot tears well up in my eyes, but then I think maybe Daddy wanted a boy.

15

Another Thing Goes Missing

Poncho is gone. It was his pink thingy always sticking out. Me laughing, "Look. He's dancing."

My mother and the-man-we've-married tell me he went to live on a farm with lots of other dogs to play with. I'm a little kid who hasn't heard that story before.

Although, I suspect it was my mother's idea, I blame the-man-we've-married.

Shout at him, "My daddy wouldn't do that!"

They buy me a yellow parakeet because yellow is my favorite color. I teach it to say its name. It flies free and poops all over the house squawking, "Twerpie. Twerpie." I try not to love it too much.

16

At the Stroke of Midnight

In my fantasies, my father is Prince Charming and Superman. As handsome as James Bond. As powerful as the president.

It's my fourteenth birthday and we are going to see him. Mom buys me a new dress, black chiffon. It's too old for me, but she doesn't say no. She never says no. I line my eyes and paint my lips. I wind my hair into a French twist so I look grown up.

When Daddy left us, I was just a little girl, and my mother was crying and my grandmother was saying, "You knew he wasn't a family man when you married him."

I look in the mirror. The little girl stares back.

Mom and I drive to the nearby town where he lives. We park in front of a Payless shoe store wedged between a dry cleaners and a nail salon.

"What are we doing?" I ask

Inside, my mother's hand is on my back, gently pushing me toward a man who is thin and balding and on his knees fitting a shoe to the foot of a seated woman.

He sees us in the doorway and rises. Though nothing like my dreams, I still want to run into his arms, but they never open.

17

What We Want To Be

I lie on my bed, chewing Bazooka bubble gum and reading the latest issue of "Millie the Model" comics. On the back is an ad for "Mark Eden Bust Developer." I've saved almost enough.

I step into the pages, in front of the lights and cameras, and it's my face on the cover of Vogue, on billboards all across the country posing with cars, cigarettes, Coca-Cola. I fly off to Rome and Paris with my movie star friends, and everybody loves me.

My dad sees me everywhere he looks. He tells anyone who will listen that he's my father, but no one believes him. When he calls, I'm too busy to answer.

18

The Boy I Like

I'm coming out of the library when I see him go into the boys' bathroom. Everyone else is in class. The halls are empty. His arms bulge under his letter jacket. I imagine them crushing me to his chest, his hands under my blouse, my skirt. Two years my senior, the-boy-I-like has never given me a waking glance.

I linger outside the door, drop my books to the ground and pretend to be picking them up. My hands shake. My breath a kite ripped loose in the wind.

When he comes out, I jump up and flash him my brightest smile.

He has no idea who I am, but he swaggers over to me, and oh-my-God his eyelashes are two inches long. His foot brushes against one of my books, but he makes no move to pick it up. His eyes travel the length of my body settling on my chest.

"Those things real?" he says, laughing as he walks away.

My face afire, I want to die. But then I think maybe that means he likes me and for the rest of the day and into the night, I play the scene over and over in my head searching for hidden meanings.

19

The Boy Who Likes Me

The-boy-who-likes-me hangs around my locker like he has some reason to be there when his locker is all the way across campus. He pushes a swath of dark hair off his face and smiles in a way that all my friends say is totally adorable.

"We're just friends," I insist.

I pull out history and math books. He takes them from my arms and walks me to my class even though it makes him late for his own.

The-boy-who-likes-me plays guitar. He gives me a Bob Dylan tape.

The-boy-who-likes-me calls me his girlfriend in front of his friends and doesn't care if they tease him.

"I wish you wouldn't do that," I say.

The-boy-who-likes-me phones nearly every night. Mom thinks it's sweet.

Sometimes, I tell Mom to say I'm not home.

20

Fault Lines

The-girl-who-is-not-my-sister graduates from high school and moves out. Sometimes I would glue her perfume bottles to the top of the dresser we shared just to get her attention. She never thought it was funny. Still, when our parents fought she'd let me crawl into bed with her.

My grandmother was wrong about my

mom and the-man-we've-married being a "good match."

Mom's a silk suit woman. He's a blue collar guy. He has dirt under his fingernails, but he brings her his check every week. His boots track in mud, but they're there. They're always there. His only real fault is that he's not my dad.

Mom sleeps in their bedroom alone. The-man-we've-married sleeps on a couch in the garage-turned-den.

Cocktail hour starts earlier every day.

"I married him for you," Mom says to me.

21

Final Exit

"**Y**our father is dying," Mom says.

"You should go," Mom says.

"Say goodbye," Mom says.

I imagine him alone, his thin frame gowned in worn cotton, hooked up to plastic tubes carrying fluids in and out of his body.

"Did he ask for me?"

"You should go."

22

Jayne with a "y"

I wander the make-up counters in Macy's, paint my face with free samples, eager to erase my own. Plain Jane. The name that has taunted me all my life. Plain. Never enough.

Across the street is the hospital where my mother sits alone by my father's bedside. It seems fitting their time together should end as it began, without me.

Ice blue eye shadow, deep cherry lips, cheeks a bold rose make me feel beautiful. Make me feel desired. I decide right then to add a "Y" to my name, like Jayne Mansfield. And just like that, Jane is gone.

23

Condolences

Mom and I sit out in the backyard sharing her pack of Salems, sending smoke rings into the moonless night.

"The military will bury him," she says.

Everything my father owned fits into one cardboard box that Mom retrieves from his motel room: Personal papers, cufflinks, photos of him and Mom before I came along.

The flame on her cigarette casts an

orange glow over her face each time she inhales. She's somewhere else. Maybe on their first date. Maybe their wedding day.

I put my arms around her, say "I'm sorry for your loss."

24

What Boys Want

I wobble outside over to the bushes afterwards and puke. A concoction of Bali-Hai, Coors, and whatever was in that last guy's flask dribbles from my chin down the front of my blouse finding its way into my padded bra. I slide to the ground shivering against a tree. The party goes on inside without me. Another Friday night cruising Stanford fraternities. Maybelline makes me look older. Makes me look sexy. Makes college boys think I know stuff. I want them to like me. They always say they will call, but they never do.

25

On My Own

A pathway winds through a forest at the edge of the ocean. Sea air wraps me in its salty essence as waves caress the shore below. I've been here before in another dream, but this time I'm not afraid. The forest morphs into a city landscape, the street where I lived when Daddy left. The bell of a cable car rings out.

And then I am by your side. Barely five years old, you stand at the window watching our father walk away. A heart drawn in the mist of your breath on the glass is beginning to melt. You turn your eyes to meet mine.

"You were supposed to take care of me," you say.

26

Just Like In the Movies

At 19, I'm the last girl I know who's still a virgin and I'm glad to get it over with. His touch is gentle and he doesn't expect me to blow him. I make all the appropriate sounds of satisfaction I've learned from watching movies. But his kisses and the cradling of his arms around me are what feed my hunger.

It doesn't matter that he's twenty years older, that he's someone else's husband, someone else's father. I tell myself I'm in love. I tell myself he loves me back.

He buys me perfume. The expensive stuff. "Joy," by Jean Pateu. And a stuffed Snoopy Dog that I sleep with every night, playing out our future together on the screen in my head like a Julia Roberts movie.

27

The Dating Game

As I watch the show, it's me I imagine on the stage with Jim Lange, sitting with my legs crossed demurely at my ankles, skirt showing just enough thigh to tease without looking slutty.

The stage lights blind me from seeing the audience, but I can hear the cheers when Jim says, "What about it folks? Will one of our bachelors be the man of her dreams?"

I think about my dreams and the men in them and they never have any faces, but they always smell of the same cloves and pine cologne.

In my hands, the index card that holds my one carefully printed question.

"Bachelor Number One," I say. "Will you be my daddy?"

28

And Then There Were None

Mom lies on the couch with a hot water bottle on her stomach even though outside the summer's heat has risen to ninety-two degrees. It's the pain again, but she says "It's nothing." When the bleeding starts the-man-we've-married makes her see the doctor. At thirteen years old, I look up the words *cervix, radiation, prognosis.*

Six years later, the cancer has found a

new place to hide. Its tentacles wrap around her lower spine, claim her for its own. I hear the word *inoperable*. I don't have to look it up.

29

Unspoken

Her phone rings, rings.

"Hi, this is Franny. Leave a message."

I hang up.

It has been years since I've heard her voice, years since we joined pinkies on the branch of her backyard tree and pledged best friends forever. Neither of us aware of the power of time to pull apart the promises of children. It's that time I want to return to now.

I consider calling again. "Hi, Franny. My mom died." Except I haven't been able to say the words out loud yet.

30

Madly in Love — Again

*H*e sits in the corner of the recording studio where I work, oozing sexuality, a giant of the rock music world. I fumble my quarter into the soda machine coin slot, press "Orange Crush" when I mean to press "Coke." I've feigned indifference toward him for weeks, while inside me exists a world where we are wed and I have his child – a girl, tall, with his black curly hair and eyes like cobalt pools.

I wear a short, tight skirt, my thighs exposed like ripe fruit. The soft leather of my boots hug my spindly calves, their laces crisscrossed two at a time, left-right-left, like I'd done so many times with roller skates, discarded now as I race to embrace grown-up pleasures. I feel his gaze on my flesh like an army of ants. Does he speak? Do I? I don't remember. At some point his lips, soft, full, and tasting of tequila press hard against mine, and that night he is in my bed.

I've imagined this moment a hundred times: *Our bodies meld together and he is mine alone and forever.* I recall every dog-eared page, perform every underlined sentence from my well-worn copy of *The Sensuous Woman*, finding my pleasure in his. Because if I'm good enough, if I can just be good enough...

Alone, still drenched in his sweat, I shiver against the cold, slip into a long, flannel nightgown, and nestle under the covers where his scent of English Leather and musk still lingers.

On the floor lie my boots, unlaced and tossed in a corner.

31

Cosmic Fluke

He slipped into my life when I had my guard down. Just another one-nighter, I'd thought.

Now we're in a U-Haul barreling down Highway 5 from San Francisco to Los Angeles, all our belongings already cohabitating in the back. We pretend we're Bonnie and Clyde on the run heading to our hideout, a tiny Beachwood

Drive apartment just below the Hollywood sign.

His dog sits in the space behind our seats, licks my ear.

We sing "Ob-la-di, ob-la-da, life goes on, ba!" and fill our bellies with Taco Bell.

His long blond curls brush against his shoulders. At six-foot-three to my five-foot-four, I call him my "Bear." He calls me "Cutie-Pie." Says he loves me. I say I love him. It all feels like a cosmic fluke.

I will be a writer, he a director. I've never lived with a guy before and I have no script.

A highway sign at an off-ramp reads "Go back. You are going the wrong way."

32

Implosion

All the boxes aren't even unpacked yet. We're still negotiating closet space. On the dining table, the remnants of dinner, another elaborate recipe from *The Joy of Cooking* I've made as I try to act out the role of the happy homemakers I've seen on TV.

The-man-I-live-with leaves messages for me with our answering service during the day. The operators giggle, "He says he loves you."

The-man-I-live-with buys me cards, not just for my birthday, sometimes for no occasion at all, just because.

The-man-I-live-with holds me in his arms after making love until I fall asleep.

The-man-I-live-with and I are sitting on the sofa watching TV, his arm around my shoulder, strong, solid, safe, when I feel my body stiffen. What feels like a flurry of wings erupts inside my chest. I can't catch my breath. A voice from inside me screaming *Run away! Run away!*

"What's wrong?" he asks.

"I don't think I love you."

33

That's A Wrap

After six months, seated at our favorite restaurant high atop the Hollywood skyline, the-man-I-live-with tells me he's leaving. He hates L.A. Misses his parents, brother and sisters. I have no frame of reference.

He takes the new Sony Trinitron, leaving me with my old black-and-white Motorola. I have to whack it on its side to keep the picture from rolling.

For weeks after, I find strands of his blond hair in our bed, on the bathroom floor, tucked between pillows on the sofa. I collect them in a jelly jar. Set it in the window where they glisten in the sun like a crown.

In his absence, he acquires the sheen of perfection, while a reel of my countless fuck-ups plays on an endless loop.

Whack. Whack.

34

Just Like Elizabeth Taylor

*E*lizabeth Taylor is getting married again. This time to some guy she met while drying out from another bout with the booze. She looks great. Really slimmed down at Betty Ford's. The newscast shows helicopters swarming over Michael Jackson's Neverland Ranch where giant white tents shelter those pretending they don't want to be seen.

I've lost track of how many husbands

she's had. She trades them in like baseball cards. This could be number six. Maybe seven. When you're Elizabeth Taylor you can have your pick of men. Even if they belong to Debbie Reynolds or Sybil Burton. Men don't say no to Liz, and they don't leave her either. It must be those violet eyes. Note to self: Get contact lenses.

35

Father Figure

My writing teacher tells me my work lacks emotion, that I need to be more in touch with my feelings and gives me the name of a therapist that works with his students. I don't tell him I've been doing my best to stay out of touch with those things for most of my life. Still, I want to be a writer. Or I don't. I don't know. I say I'll go. For a month. Months later I'm still there.

The-woman-who-is-my-therapist sits in a chair embroidered in the plumage of peacocks. I sit facing her in its twin. They are the only things of color in an otherwise austere office and I wonder if they're supposed to create some type of bonding experience between us.

I joke with her, "If it weren't for bad relationships, I would have no relationships at all."

She doesn't laugh. Tough audience.

"Last week you were telling me about your mother's boyfriend, Sam."

"It was no big deal. I don't know why I even brought it up," I say.

I reach for my coffee, long grown cold. The silence between us amasses like an ocean swell pulling me under. And there is Sam. And there is the rock star, and the married guy and all the others surrounding me in the surf, until they drift away leaving only one. And there is my father.

"I just wanted him to love me," I finally manage to say.

"Was that how you believed a father would behave?" she asks.

"How would I know?"

36

And Then We Are One

Afloat in a vodka-induced slumber, still dressed for seduction, the Other Woman wanders the halls of a house that feels known to her. Somewhere, a baby cries. The hallway opens onto a living room, where the scent of cloves and pine, her father's cologne, slaps her senses, but he is nowhere in sight. A baby girl, red-faced and crying, lies alone in a playpen.

The Other Woman picks her up, holds

her close to her heart and soothes her tears until the baby's body relaxes and rests peacefully in her arms.

"It wasn't your fault," the Other Woman whispers. "None of it. It was never your fault."

37

Seismic Shift

A violent shaking jars me awake. In the darkness, dishes fly from cupboards and shatter. A lamp crashes to the floor. Bookcases topple over. Through it all, a loud roar like a train engine bears down upon me. I grip the blankets, pull them over my head. Twenty long seconds later the 6.7 Northridge earthquake has laid ruin to much of my northern Los Angeles neighborhood.

My building is one of the lucky ones that has not collapsed, but frequent and severe aftershocks over the coming days will prove its resilience to be much stronger than my own. Two weeks later, my trusted Volvo packed with my belongings exits Highway 101 at Santa Barbara and carries me into the mountains high above the city's red-tiled rooftops. The two-lane road snakes its way toward a sky so clear that at night the stars put on a celestial lightshow of such grandeur as to call the most fallen back to God.

Below, hills lush with new spring grass and old-growth oaks roll across the valley floor where horses, new foals at their sides, peacefully graze. A ridge of mountains encircles this land like a mother holding it in her protective arms. It is here that my heart will heal.

A red-tail hawk dips down in front of my windshield as if beckoning me to follow. In Native American lore, red-tails are divine messengers who bring guidance from the heavens and arrange the changes necessary to prompt our spiritual growth. A psychic once told me that the hawk was my spirit animal.

In that same psychic reading, she told me that my father was coming through.

"He wants you to know that he knows what he missed," she said.

I think back now to the time of his dying and how, in anger, I withheld the love from him in death that he had withheld from me in life.

Me, too, Dad. Me, too.

Acknowledgements

Thank you to my writing tribe: Gay Degani, April Bradley, Lori Sambol Brody, and Lynn Mundell for their friendship and support through the writing of this book, and a whole lot of "you got this" texts when I wavered.

To Robert Scotellaro for having more faith in me than I often have in myself, and reminding me that the words come when you "show up."

Many thanks to Meg Pokrass, whose workshop based on her novella-in-flash, "The Loss Detector," provided the book's structure and coaxed so many long-buried memories from their hiding places into the light where they no long wield power over me.

To the editors of *South Shore Review* for publishing "At the Stroke of Midnight," *New Flash Fiction Review* for publishing "Just the Two of Us," and *Sledgehammer Lit* for publishing "Ode to the Lone Sperm."

To Lori Hettler, publicist extraordinaire. Thank you for taking another trip around the sun with me, my friend.

Miette Gillette and the Whiskey Tit team, thank you for bringing my story into the world and for the care and respect with which you have treated it.

Most of all, thank you to my mother for teaching me that I could achieve anything I set my mind to, that even in what appeared to be a road's end there was "always a way." Gone too soon for me to understand that you did your very best, and to tell you that I am grateful. I miss you every day, Mom.

About the Author

Photo: Patty Wilding

Jayne Martin's writing career began with a twenty-year stint writing movies-for television. Her credits include "Big

Spender" for Animal Planet and "A Child Too Many," "Cradle of Conspiracy" and "Deceived By Trust" for Lifetime. She has been the recipient of the following honors: Fall 2013 Women-On-Writing Flash Fiction Winner; 2016 New Millennium Writings Flash Fiction Finalist; 2016 Vestal Review VERA Award; 2017 Pushcart Nominee; 2018 Best Small Fictions Nominee. 2019 Best Microfiction Nominee. Her book of humor essays, "Suitable for Giving: A Collection of Wit with A Side of Wry," was published in 2011. Her collection of microfiction, "Tender Cuts," from Vine Leaves Press was published in 2019. She currently lives near Santa Barbara, California where she rides horses and drinks copious amounts of fine wine, though not at the same time. www.jaynemartin-writer.com

About the Publisher

Whisk(e)y Tit is committed to restoring degradation and degeneracy to the literary arts. We work with authors who are unwilling to sacrifice intellectual rigor, unrelenting playfulness, and visual beauty in our literary pursuits, often leading to texts that would otherwise be abandoned in today's largely homogenized literary landscape. In a world governed by idiocy, our commitment to these principles is an act of civil service and civil disobedience alike.

CPSIA information can be obtained
at www.ICGtesting.com
Printed in the USA
BVHW042255060422
633508BV00008B/237

9 781952 600258